KU-195-731

Food around the world

The Caribbean

Polly Goodman

WAYLAND

First published in 2006 by Wayland

First published in paperback in 2009

Reprinted in 2009 by Wayland

Wayland
Hachette Children's Books
338 Euston Road, London NW1 3BH

Copyright © 2006 Wayland

The right of Polly Goodman to be identified as
the author of this work as been asserted by her
in accordance with the Copyright, Designs and
Patents Act, 1988.

All rights reserved.

Editor: Sarah Gay
Designer: Tim Mayer
Consultant: Susannah Blake

British Library Cataloguing in Publication Data
Goodman, Polly
    The Caribbean. - (Food around the world)
    1.Food habits - Caribbean Area - Juvenile literature
    2.Cookery, Caribbean - Juvenile literature
    3.Caribbean Area   - Social life and customs - Juvenile
    literature
    I.Title
    394.1'2'09729

ISBN: 978-0-7502-5861-6

Wayland is a division of Hachette Children's Books,
an Hachette UK Company.
www.hachette.co.uk

Cover photograph: a colourful street market
in Grenada.

Photo credits: Lonely Planet/Michael Lawrence 6,
Steve Winter/Getty Images 8, Wayland Picture Library
9, Simon Reddy/Alamy 10, Robert Harding Picture
Library Ltd/Alamy 11, Greg Johnston/Danita Delimont
12 , 17, 22 and title page, M. Timothy O'Keefe/Alamy 13,
Lonely Planet/Jerry Alexander 14, 18, 19, 20 and 21, Paul
Thomas/Danita Delimont 15, Richard Bradbury/Getty
Images 16 and cover, eStock/Pictures Colour Library 23,
Andrew Sydenham/Anthony Blake Photo Library 24,
Franz-Marc Frei/CORBIS 25, Lew Robertson/Jupiter
Images 26.

The website addresses (URLs) included in this book were
valid at the time of going to press. However, because of
the nature of the Internet, it is possible that some
addresses may have changed, or sites may have changed
or closed down since publication. While the author and
publisher regret any inconvenience this may cause the
readers, no responsibility for any such changes can be
accepted by either the author or the publisher.

Contents

Words in **bold** can be found in the glossary on page 28

Welcome to the Caribbean

The Caribbean is made up of thousands of islands in the Caribbean Sea. It includes countries such as Cuba, Jamaica and Puerto Rico.

People from all over the world have brought their own traditions and cooking styles to the Caribbean. Today, Caribbean food is a delicious mixture of many different flavours.

▼ *Over the last 500 years, people from many different countries have settled in the Caribbean.*

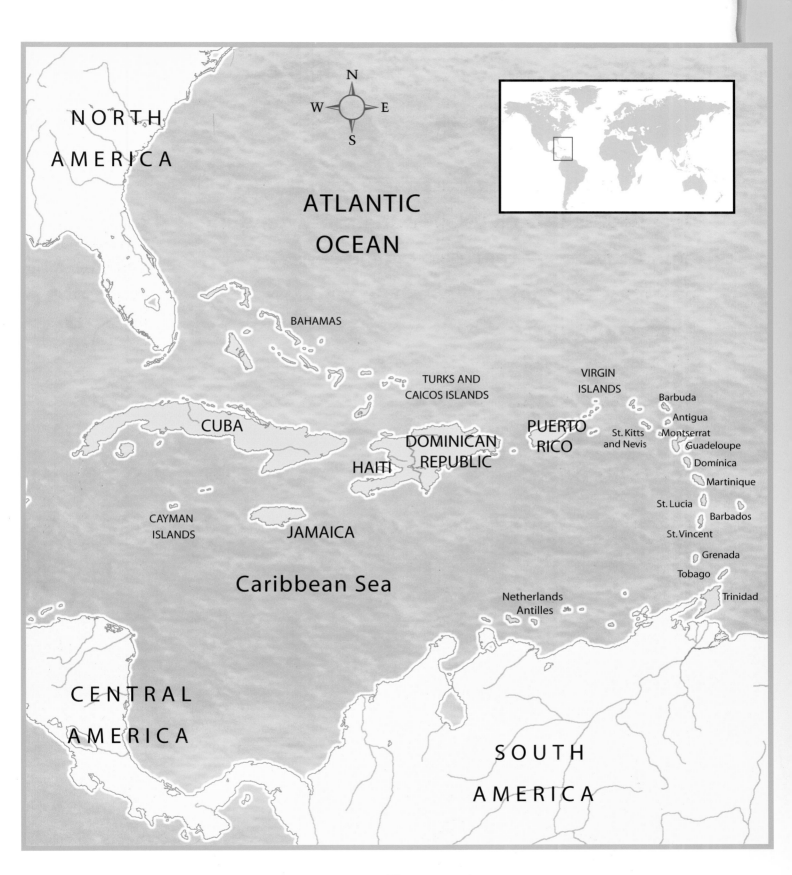

NORTH
AMERICA

ATLANTIC
OCEAN

BAHAMAS

TURKS AND
CAICOS ISLANDS

VIRGIN
ISLANDS

CUBA

Barbuda

Antigua

PUERTO
RICO

St. Kitts
and Nevis

Montserrat

Guadeloupe

DOMINICAN
REPUBLIC

HAITI

Domínica

Martinique

CAYMAN
ISLANDS

St. Lucia

Barbados

JAMAICA

St. Vincent

Caribbean Sea

Grenada

Tobago

Netherlands
Antilles

Trinidad

CENTRAL

AMERICA

SOUTH

AMERICA

▲ *The Caribbean islands are marked in orange. They stretch over*
4,000 km off the coasts of North and South America.

Farming and weather

The Caribbean has a tropical climate, which means it is hot all year round. Between June and November there is a rainy season. Plants need rain and sunshine to grow, so food crops grow well there.

▼ *Many different vegetables grow on this vegetable farm in Cuba.*

Food fact

Most people in the Caribbean grow fruit or vegetables in their own gardens.

◄ Every banana tree grows a single bunch of between 50 and 150 bananas.

Many crops such as sugar cane, rice, bananas, coffee and spices are grown on big farms called **plantations**. Most of the crops grown on plantations are sold at supermarkets in countries all over the world.

Rice, bread and spices

Rice is served at almost every Caribbean meal. In Cuba, yellow rice is made with saffron, a yellow spice. Many different types of bread are also eaten. **Roti** and **dhalpourri** are Indian flat breads that are popular in Trinidad.

◀ The Jamaican dish, rice and peas, is made with coconut, milk and spices.

Spices are very important in Caribbean cooking. Nutmeg is the most common spice in Grenada, while pimento is popular in Jamaica. Chilli peppers are used to make hot pepper sauces on the island of Puerto Rico.

▲ Spices add flavour and colour to Caribbean food.

Food fact

Before people had fridges, spices covered the taste of meat that had gone bad in the heat.

Fruit and vegetables

The Caribbean is famous for its exotic fruits, such as pineapples, **ackee** and **guava**. Coconut is used in breads, cakes, ice cream, drinks and sauces. **Plantains** look a bit like bananas, but they are cooked before they are eaten.

◀ *These women in Grenada are carrying trays of mangoes and* **breadfruit** *to sell to tourists.*

Vegetables are the main foods of the Caribbean and are made into stews, soups or curries. **Yams** are baked, fried, or boiled like potatoes. **Cassava** can be ground and made into flour.

▲ *In Honduras, bread made from cassava flour is baked over a fire.*

Food fact

Coconut water, carrot punch, **soursop** juice and banana milkshake are popular Caribbean drinks.

Fish and meat

On the Caribbean coast people eat fresh seafood such as crab, **conch** and shark. Fish can be barbecued, stewed or curried. Fish used to be **preserved** in salt, and salted fish is still part of many Caribbean dishes, such as ackee and saltfish.

▼ Ackee and saltfish is eaten for breakfast in Jamaica.

Chicken, goat and pork are popular types of meat. They are usually cooked in stews or curries. Meat is often eaten '**jerk**' style, which is coated in a spicy mixture and slowly cooked in a pit or barbecued.

◀ *This man sells conch shells in Grenada.*

Food fact

Pickled pigs' trotters are a popular dish in Trinidad.

Shopping and street food

Every town in the Caribbean has a busy market, where fresh fruit, vegetables, fish, chickens and eggs are sold. Every village and town has a bakery selling bread, and a general store selling household goods.

▼ *This busy street market is selling all kinds of fruit and vegetables.*

Street food is very popular in the Caribbean. Most busy streets have mobile stalls selling ice cream, banana chips or freshly roasted peanuts. Other stalls serve roasted corn, barbecued chicken, hot peppered shrimp and fried fish.

▲ An oil drum has been made into a barbecue to cook jerk chicken at this stall.

Mealtimes in the Caribbean

Everyday Caribbean meals might include dishes from the menus below.

Breakfast

Corn porridge
Ackee and saltfish
Banana bread
Tropical fruit salad
Cereal

———————

Coffee
Fresh pineapple juice

Lunch

Grilled jerk chicken
Five-spice roast chicken
Grilled, **marinated** fish

———————

Coffee flan

———————

Ginger beer
Fresh watermelon juice

▶ A dish of jerk chicken, ackee and saltfish, goat meat and fried plantains.

◀ A Cuban family eat a meal together.

Dinner

Callaloo soup

Pick-up saltfish (dried, salted cod and chilli with a lime dressing)

Deep-fried saltfish in batter with a hot pepper sauce

Tomato and coconut fish stew

Curried goat with rice

Rum and chocolate pudding

Coconut ice cream

Coffee

Around the islands

Caribbean food is a mixture of cooking styles from all over the world. Cuban cooking uses a mixture of Spanish, African and Mexican foods. Jamaica, Barbados and Grenada have more African dishes.

▼ **Tamales** is a Mexican dish that is popular in Cuba.

Martinique, Haiti and St Lucia were once controlled by the French, so there are many French dishes. Trinidad has the largest number of Asian **immigrants**, so curries and other Indian dishes are popular.

▲ Gumbo, an African soup, is prepared on a Jamaican beach.

Special occasions

Every Saturday, it is traditional to make a big soup for lunch using leftover vegetables from the week. On Sundays, most families share a big lunch of roast chicken or a curry.

◄ This street vendor is serving a plate of fried dough balls with pineapple at a fishing festival in St Lucia.

These girls are wearing traditional costumes for a carnival parade in Guadeloupe. Most islands celebrate carnival in February each year.

The biggest celebration of the year on each Caribbean island is carnival. It is celebrated on most islands with street parades and roadside food stalls. Fried chicken, chilled coconut water and sweet tamarind balls are sold by street **vendors**.

Festival food

Most people in the Caribbean are Christians. There are also many Hindus and Muslims, and people who follow traditional African religions. Every religious celebration involves eating special food.

◀ Christian families enjoy a special Christmas pudding together.

At Christmas, Christians eat whole roast pig, goat or turkey. At Easter, grilled fish and Easter buns (spicy cakes) are enjoyed.

Phagwa is a festival celebrated by Hindus in the Caribbean. Many Hindus are **vegetarian**, so vegetarian dishes such as pumpkin, curried potatoes and eggplant with rice and dahl are eaten.

▲ Hindus in Trinidad spray coloured powder on each other at Phagwa.

25

Make a banana milkshake!

What you need

4 bananas

200 ml vanilla ice cream

100 ml milk

$\frac{1}{2}$ teaspoon nutmeg

What to do

1. Peel the bananas and cut them into thick slices.
2. Put all the ingredients into a food processor or blender.
3. Blend the ingredients until smooth.
4. Pour the milkshake into two glasses and serve with straws.

Ask an adult to help you make this milkshake and always be careful with sharp knives.

A balanced diet

This food pyramid shows which foods you should eat to have a healthy, **balanced diet**.

We shouldn't eat too many fats, oils, cakes or sweets.

Milk, cheese, meat, fish, beans and eggs help to keep us strong.

We should eat plenty of vegetables and fruit to keep healthy.

Bread, cereal, rice and pasta should make up most of our diet.

Caribbean meals use all foods from the pyramid. Some Caribbean dishes are fried in oil but most are made from rice, fruit and vegetables, with some meat, fish or beans, which helps to balance Caribbean diets.

Glossary

ackee a red and cream fruit that grows on trees

balanced diet a diet that includes a mixture of different foods, which supply all the things a body needs to keep healthy

breadfruit a large, round fruit that is usually served as a vegetable

cassava a vegetable that can be ground into flour

conch a shellfish that has sweet, pink meat inside

dhalpourri an Indian bread seasoned with split peas

guava a round fruit with a thin, yellow skin

immigrant someone who moves to a new country to live

marinated soaked in a savoury sauce to add flavour

Phagwa a Hindu festival celebrating the triumph of good over evil

pickled food that is kept in vinegar to stop it going bad

plantain a vegetable that looks like a banana

plantation a large farm where crops are grown to be sold abroad

preserved kept from going bad

jerk a style of cooking where meat or fish is covered in spices and cooked on a barbecue

roti a type of Indian flat bread

soursop a green fruit with a spiny skin

tamales parcels of meat or beans wrapped in corn pancakes and steamed

vegetarian a person who does not eat meat or fish

vendor a seller

yam a vegetable that can be steamed, boiled, mashed, grilled, roasted or fried

Further information

Books to read

A Flavour of the Caribbean by Linda Illsley (Wayland, 2006)
Changing Face of the Caribbean by Ali Brownlie (Wayland, 2006)
Facts About Countries: The Caribbean by Ian Graham (Watts, 2005)
Let's Eat! What Children Eat Around the World by Beatrice Hollyer (Frances Lincoln, 2005)
Letters from Around the World: Jamaica by Ali Brownlie (Evans, 2009)
We Come from Jamaica by Ali Brownlie (Wayland, 2002)

Websites

CIA Factbook
www.cia.gov/library/publications/the-world-factbook/index.html
Facts and figures about Jamaica and other countries in the Caribbean

Geocities: Caribbean Culture
www.geocities.cmo/shandycan/jamaicanrecipes.html

Jamaicans.com
www.jamaicans.com
Everything to do with Jamaica, including recipes

Jamaica Tourist Board
www.visitjamaica.com
What to see and where to go in Jamaica, including recipes

Index

All the numbers in **bold** refer to photographs.

B

Barbados 20
bread 10, 13, **13**, 18
breakfast 18

C

carnival 23, **23**
Christmas 24, **24**
climate 8
coffee 9, 18, 19
crops 8–9
curry 13, 14, 15, 21, 22
Cuba 6, 8, **8**, 19, **19**, 20

D

dinner 19
drinks 13, 18, 19, 23, 26, **26**

E

Easter 24

F

fish (see seafood)
fruit 8, 9, **9**, 12, **12**, 16, 17, **18**, 19, 22, **22**, 26, 27

G

Grenada 11, 12, **12**, 15, **15**, 20

Guadeloupe 23, **23**
Guayana 25

H

Haiti 21
Honduras 13, **13**

J

Jamaica 6, 11, 14, 20, 21, **21**
jerk 14, 17, **17**, 18, **18**

L

lunch 18, 22

M

market 16, **16**
Martinique 21
meat 11, 15, 17, **17**, 18, **18**, 22, 23, 24

P

Phagwa 25, **25**
plantations 9
Puerto Rico 6, 11

R

religion 24–25
rice 9, 10, **10**, 19, 25, 27

S

seafood 14, **14**, 15, **15**, 16, 17, 18, **18**, 19, 24, 27

shops 9, 16
soups 19, 21, **21**
spices 9, 11, **11**, 18, 19
St Lucia 21
sugar cane 9

T

Trinidad 10, 15, 21, 22, **22**, 25, **25**

V

vegetables 8, **8**, 13, **13**, 16, **16**, 17, 22, 25, 27

30